Why Do Boys...?

A HEART-TO-HEART CONVERSATION
ABOUT UNDERSTANDING
BOYS AND MEN WHO NEVER GREW UP.

By PANTA A. WILSON
Author of 100 Ghetto Golden Rules

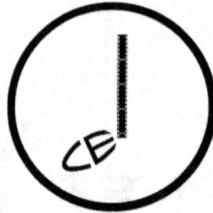

CIRCLE OF ENTERTAINMENT INC.

PO BOX 25091 BROOKLYN, NY 11202
OFFICE 718-930-4220

Copyright © 2010
Published By

Ceipub Division Of Circle Of Entertainment Incorporated

Credits
Illustration And Design By James Paul

Acknowledgments
L. Aldridge, N. Charles, C. Rousseau, M. Stewart, R. Stuart

Made And Printed In The U.S.A.

ISBN-13: 978-0-9845320-1-8
ISBN-10: 0-9845320-1-3

This book is dedicated in memory of

Lamont R. Bishop

Table of Contents

INTRODUCTION

Why do boys...? This is an age old question that never seems to go away. Within each generation, it seems to find a way to regenerate and penetrate itself back into society's social networks. Conversations about why boys do the things they do can be heard in bedrooms between mothers and daughters; at the spa amongst girlfriends; in the classrooms; on the train; in blogs and talk shows. It's everywhere and it is armed with an uninhibited resilience. There is no wrong place or wrong time.

Honey, it's 3 am. I don't know why I always leave the toilet seat up but can we discuss it in the morning?

Now, some of you women are thinking to yourself, "Well technically, it *is* the morning". If so, then you have admittedly reinforced my point. If religion is the gold recipient, then "Why do boys...?" would certainly place silver for being one of the most heated and controversial topics of debate.

After many years of being in the hot-seat and going to battle with close female friends and a few hostile strangers over the topic of "Why do boys...?", I decided it was finally time to publicly address and dissect some of the topics I have come across throughout the years, with a no ice and no chaser approach. Now, certainly some folks will disagree with my philosophy, my reasoning and my advice. Some may even be offended. Others may question my qualifications and expertise. Well, let me take a moment to address those concerns. First of all, I am not a psychologist nor am I attempting to answer the question of "Why do boys...?" from a technical or clinical approach.

The purpose of this book is to have an open, heart-to-heart conversation. I simply wanted to recreate those nights where my female friends came over and we sat Indian style in my living room. We would talk until sunrise about why boys do the things they do. It would often end with one of us asking the other, "Why are you yelling?" The reply would be something like, "I am not yelling! I am just passionately talking! I can't help that my voice gets higher and louder when I am passionate about something!" Sadly enough, I have to admit it wasn't just the girls who were yelling at a high pitch. At the beginning of the night, I was Barry White but by the end, I had somehow turned into Alvin and the chipmunks covering a Mariah Carey song.

It's funny, but as far as I can remember, I've always had a closer connection to females. Perhaps this is mainly due to my being raised by a single parent mother. In elementary school, I recall the times when the boys were constantly teasing me for hanging out with the girls during lunch time. I got called all sorts of names: sissy boy; fag; you name it! Well, luckily for me, I already knew that only sticks and stones could break my bones, so the name calling didn't really hurt me. Actually, I was quite befuddled by the irony of it all, because while the boys were getting dirty and playing tag with each other, I was playing house and landing my first kiss. At that moment, I was hooked. I made it my life-long quest to explore and understand these beautiful and fascinating creatures. On that very day, I declared "I love girls!" Later in life, I discovered that my pre-adolescent declaration and over-zealousness for girls would take me on one of the most tumultuous roller coaster rides that life had to offer.

Let's examine another one of life's interesting equations; a single parent household is equivalent to a single income household, which in turn equals a single bedroom apartment in a low income neighborhood with a high ratio of crime. This equation gives you a generalized glimpse at my home town of Brooklyn, New York, and the environment I grew up in. For neighbors, I had murderers; drug dealers; pimps; hustlers; drug addicts; thieves; rapists and gangsters. These were the types of characters who surrounded me. They were my classmates, my neighbors and my friends.

One day on my way to school, when I was about 13 or 14 years old, I was approached by an alleged local drug dealer. It wasn't something he advertised but I knew there was an odd situation going on, because this guy never held a job, yet he drove expensive cars and wore tons of jewelry.

"Hey kid," he said to me. "You want to make 50 dollars?"

Now, to a poor kid from the hood, 50 dollars sounded more like 50 thousand dollars. I was like, "Yeah! What do I have to do?"

"All I need you to do is take this brown paper bag," he said. "You see that guy standing over there? Hand it to him. And don't open it!"

I said, "OK" and delivered the bag he'd given me. My 50 bucks and I were on the way to school with a big ole smile. I was intrigued and amazed at how quickly and easily I made 50 dollars. It didn't even take five minutes. On the opposing end, there lay my guidance counselor, telling me about summer jobs that paid five dollars an hour. At that moment, there was no comparison. Of course, at that time, I had no clue about the consequences of making fast-money. I never knew exactly what was in that bag but I suspect it had been my first unknowing participation in an illegal activity. Growing up, I continued experimenting and dabbling in more illegal activities and eventually I learned what those consequences were.

The turning point happened when I was 13. All at once, I was hit with the realization that I was poor and I did not like it! In fact, I took it pretty hard! The flood gates of my reality opened and I became very angry at my misfortune. Soon, my self pity and

"Why me, Lord?" woes turned into an aggressive "By any means" mantra. By any means, I was going to be rich. By any means, I was going to get out of the hood.

I was starting to feel imprisoned and, like most inmates, I began to fantasize about an escape route. My mother used to force me to attend church. Her idea of escape was to believe in God and have faith. My elders preached that excelling in education was the only way out. Then you had the 'streets' master-plans of escape, which was to either become a professional athlete, a rapper or engage in some sort of illegal, fast-money hustle. I didn't want to limit my options, so I decided I would engage in all of the aforementioned routes equally and with immense conviction. I prayed; I wrote poetry and songs; I was on my school's basketball team; I graduated magna cum laude with a bachelor degree in business administration, and yes, I engaged in a slew of illegal activities.

One of the first things that landed for me was music. I had gotten a record deal with a major label and created a hit song, all before the age of 21. I received my first RIAA gold record, commemorating over 500,000 copies sold. The lifestyle change was amazing. Whereas I had once been blown away by making 50 dollars in 5 minutes, now I was being paid 5,000 dollars to perform a 3 minute song. This was the catalyst which granted me the opportunity to socialize and do business with some of the most powerful, wealthiest entrepreneurs and entertainers in the world.

From roach and rat infested apartments to luxury condominiums and five-star hotels; from riding the filthy subways to flying in private jets; from socializing with gangsters and murderers to socializing with celebrities and business moguls. Besides the obvious fact that I'm a boy with an intrinsic advantage, it is truly my extremely diversified background and accumulation of worldly experiences that allows me to have such a profound insight into "Why do boys"?

Then it came time to actually start writing the

book *Why do boys...?* Lets see. Where do I start?
What topics should I cover? How should I structure
the book? These were some of the questions
that were running through my mind at the time.
Well, I decided the best way to start was to hit
the pavements of New York City and directly ask
women what they wanted to know about boys.

After a few days, I realize that maybe this wasn't
the best approach. Sure, I got a few responses but
most of the women said they were in a rush and
didn't have time to stop. Others thought that when
I asked them to participate in a survey, it was just
another cheap, cheesy pick-up line. A few of the
women held tightly to their pocketbooks. I suspect
they thought I was actually trying to rob them.

Since pounding the pavements didn't quite work out, I decided to take a technological approach. I took the survey to the World Wide Web. One day, I went online and joined a majority of the popular social networking sites. My strategy was to send an email blast to women of all races, between the ages of 18 to 35, located in different parts of the world. The email stated:

Hey. I am a writer and I am doing a book on understanding "boys" for women. Just trying to get the top things women want to know, so if you don't mind, please finish the sentence, "Why do boys...?" Thanx; I really appreciate it and don't forget to add me as a friend. ☺

Surprisingly, within a short period of time, I received an overwhelming amount of responses. By the end of the survey, I had accumulated hundreds of replies from women all over the world. By the way, special thanks to all of the women that responded to my emails. It is truly appreciated. All of you are the reason and the inspiration for writing this book. Here are a few examples of actual email replies I received:

Why do boys…?

SAY THAT THEY WANT A GOOD GIRL AND THEN WHEN THEY GET ONE THEY DON'T KNOW HOW TO TREAT HER?

OK.....Why do boys lie and play games?

*WHY DO BOYS LIE AND ACT LIKE THEY
DON'T WANT A SERIOUS RELATIONSHIP
WHEN IT'S OFFERED BUT COMPLAIN THAT
THERE IS NO RIDE OR DIE FEMALES LEFT?*

*Why do boys think they run everything like
they are someone special and think they can
do and say whatever they want?*

*OK why do boys/men have a hard time
trusting?*

.......Have to have you and your whole crew?

WHY DO BOYS??? "CALL THEM SELF
PIMPS OR PLAYERS?" They thinks it's OK
for them to go out and have sex with plenty of
females and it's all good... BUT the moment a
female has sex with more than one man she's
a Hoe Or A Slut...

WHY DO GUYS TELL YOU HOW MUCH
THEY LOVE U AND HOW MUCH THEY
DON'T WANNA LIVE WITHOUT U, AND
YET THEY DON'T ACT LIKE IT AT ALL
SOMETIMES.....BUT THEN IF YOU KEEP
PUSHING THEM AWAY, THEY WON'T JUST
LET YOU GO AND LEAVE YOU ALONE

LIKE YOU MEAN A LOT TO THEM..............

.... WHY DO GUYS LIKE NAUGHTY

GIRLS??? ....WHY DO GUYS

CAN'T BE FAITHFUL SOMETIMES?............

WHY DOES A GUY FAIL TO RESIST

TEMPTATIONS IF HE REALLY LOVES A

GIRL WITH ALL HIS HEART ?.............I'M

KINDA CHILDISH IN SO MANY WAYS BUT

THESE ARE THE THINGS INSIDE MY HEAD

RIGHT NOW.....LOL...........................LAST

ONE INSIDE MY HEAD-------WHY DO GUYS

WOULDN'T WANNA LOSE YOU BUT CAN'T

STOP HURTING YOU OOOOOOOOOOOOO

OOOOOOOOOOOOOOOOOOOOOOOVER AND

OVER AGAIN? 😊

Take so long to grow up?

Leave a mother to be single and raise THEIR family?

Why do boys never understand what girls want?

Always tell you that you are beautiful no matter what you put on, how you do ur makeup, and hair? Real women do like honest feedback to help them please their man.

And lastly, one of my favorite replies to "Why do

boys...?" was an email that simply said:

Hell I don't know they just damn do !

So after reviewing and shuffling through hundreds of emails, I began the process of selecting the top ten "Why do boys...?" responses. "Cheat" and "lie" were by far the most popular responses from women who participated in this particular survey. Although my initial goal was to address topics that women were most interested in, the top ten was not solely based on popularity or ranking. Uniqueness, level of controversy and depth were also factors I used to determine what issues made the list. With that being said, the top ten "Why do boys...?" topics that will be discussed throughout *Why Do Boys...?*

are:

1. Why do boys pretend they don't like you when they do?

2. Why do boys say they want a good girl and don't know how to treat one?

3. Why do boys like bimbos?

4. Why do boys feel intimidated by successful women?

5. Why do boys lie?

6. Why do boys cheat?

7. Why do boys hit girls?

8. Why do boys rape?

9. Why do boys choose not to communicate?

10. Why do boys have a hard time trusting?

As I've mentioned before, my goal with this book

is to truly have a heart-to-heart conversation and an

open discussion amongst friends. So at this time,

I ask you to relax, make yourself comfortable, get

yourself a bottle of water or, if you prefer, a glass of

wine and settle in for a good read. Now let's talk!

CHAPTER 1

WHY DO BOYS PRETEND THEY DON'T

LIKE YOU WHEN THEY DO?

Interestingly enough, this all stems from our childhood, even before puberty and machismo kick in, when we commence with our hooting and hollering and whistling and coming up with good pick-up lines. Before all of this, girls are just foreign creatures with cooties and they're yucky. It's in every boys' club manual. Rule number one: No girls allowed! It's an honorary obligation that all members uphold this imaginary line that separates the two genders from socializing together. Girls on one side and boys on the other! While they're over there playing house with their stupid dolls, we men are playing war with our dolls. I mean 'action figures'. It's quite obvious we have absolutely nothing in common.

Even in the early stages of development, there is that certain camaraderie amongst boys whose only goal in life, at this point, is to keep our membership in the old-boys'-club active and problem free. All we want to do is fit in and preserve our cool-points. Anything that jeopardizes this is simply not an option.

Well, within seconds, tragedy struck me faster than a lightning bolt. Before you knew it, I had my first female friend. It happened to be my babysitter's daughter. We were both the same age and attended the same elementary school. Her mom would pick us up from school and I would stay at her house everyday until my mom got off from work. At first, it was super-weird, because I had this general bias towards girls. I didn't think we would have anything in common, so in the beginning, I really didn't talk much.

Contrary to my beliefs, it turned out that we had a lot more in common than I anticipated. We both enjoyed watching the same cartoons; we liked eating the same candies and she told the most hilarious Knock-Knock jokes. I guess after being struck with lightning, one of the after-effects is a tingling sensation, because that's exactly what I

felt. There was an awkward tingle that engulfed

my body. I didn't know what was happening to me.

All I knew was that it was a different experience

from when I became friends with the boys. As time

passed, we became closer and I started looking at

my friend and playmate with a new set of eyes. I

remember thinking "Wow, she's really cute", but

prior to that, I'd never paid much attention to her in

that manner.

Once I discovered how cute she was, it was

pretty much downhill from there. I had no problem

playing rough and wrestling with her but after the

'cute' factor was added, I began to worry about

hurting her. I used to take my action figures and beat

her dolls up. But once I decided she was cute, she

had me dressing her Barbies and styling their hair.

Things were progressing rapidly and, oddly enough,

I enjoyed it. I began to question why the boys'

club was so adamant about not engaging in such a

wonderful experience. It was fun and exciting and

I am pretty sure they would have enjoyed the new

games I stumbled upon, especially the infamous

"show me" game.

Now parents, if you're not familiar with this

game, you may want to take notes. The "show

me" game is pretty straight-forward. The rules are

simple; "You show me yours and I'll show you

mine". Now, there is no need to get all uptight.

We were just two innocent kids, curious about our

bodies; experimenting and discovering. Well, maybe not so innocent, because we both instinctively knew that this game had elements of danger and risk and if caught, we would probably be punished. So we cleverly and conveniently only played the "show me" game when her mom was occupied in the kitchen making us snacks or wrapped up watching her favorite soap opera.

Next to Christmas Eve, I must say that going to the babysitter was my next most anticipated event. Unfortunately, as the English proverb states, "All good things must come to an end". My friend and playmate betrayed me by crossing that imaginary line. It all happened during lunchtime, in front of my boy buddies. We were having a good old time horsing around, making noise and occasionally

throwing things at the girls' table, just to annoy

them. Out of nowhere, a girl that barely stood 4-feet

tall was towering over me like a folklore giant. In

her hands, she held onto a couple of dolls.

"Hey Panta," she blurted out "Do you want to

help me dress Keisha?"

"Keisha" was the name she'd given one of her

dolls. Girl power sure packs one hell of a punch,

because before I could blink, all of my buddies

had turned into mute quadriplegics. They just sat

there, waiting for me to respond. What a dilemma!

If I went with her, I would surely be ridiculed. If

I didn't, I was on my way to losing the friendship

with a very cool girl. Naturally, I chose what I believed was my best option, which was to deny, deny, deny!

I started off by pretending not to comprehend. "Who is Keisha? What is that?" I asked her.

She looked puzzled. "Panta, stop playing! You know who Keisha is!"

"I don't know what you're talking about" I insisted. To further support my position, I stated "I am a boy! I don't even play with dolls!"

"Fine!" she said, as she rolled her eyes and walked angrily away.

Watching her go, I already knew that things between us were no longer "fine". She was confused by my actions. She was angry. Even worse, she was hurt. My boy pals, who were all momentarily stunned, were beginning to come to. Although I'd upheld the boys' club rules by denying my female friend and pretending not to like her, I was still bombarded with a series of berating and taunting "Eewww! Panta has a girlfriend!" and "Eewww! Panta likes to play with dolls!" They laughed until their bellies hurt and tears fell from their eyes.

I was very upset at her for having broken the unspoken agreement we had. I'd seen her many times in school before then. She would wave hello and that would be all. Why did she decide on that particular day to 'out me' and openly expose our intimate behind-the-scenes relationship?

During the following weeks, we went back to not talking much, just like when we'd first met. In school, I continued to pretend that I didn't like her, in order to get back in the good graces of the other boys. I couldn't wait until I wasn't the subject of ridicule anymore. I wanted the target of teasing to shift to one of my other classmates. My denials had escalated from "I don't like her" to "I can't stand that girl!" I made her out to be some crazy girl who just randomly asked me to play with her.

One evening, she broke the ice and asked why I

was being so mean to her. Why was I saying mean things and acting like that in school? At first I told her, "I don't know" but slowly and awkwardly, I began to explain.

"It's not that I don't like you, cause I do," I said to her. "I think you're cool and I don't mind playing with you at your house but just not in school. I just don't want my friends to think I'm a girl."

All she said to me was "That's stupid", and she was absolutely right! The whole thing was stupid! The fact that one minute I was cool and the next minute I was treated like an outcast left a bitter taste in my mouth. I was about to embark on one of the most revolutionary decisions in my eight years of life. I was pumping myself up and saying "Those guys are stupid and I don't care what they think or what they say!" I was like a young soldier preparing for war. My decision was made! I was no longer ashamed and I had to make things right with my true friend. That day, I declared war! I will not be playing punch ball, tag or dodge ball with the other boys. When they asked, "Are you playing?" I'd reply "NO!" I stuck my bird's chest out, did an about-face and marched right toward a group of girls, which included my dear friend.

Nervously and timidly I asked, "Can I Play?" My friend smiled and handed me a doll.

It was over. I had crossed the enemy lines and

was prepared for the worst. As expected, the boys continued to call me names but I ignored them. In time, the name calling stopped. In fact, I had regained my cool-points and at a higher level than before, because now other boys were getting struck by lightning and they started coming to me for advice to hook up. "Hey Panta, what should I say to her?" Or "What's-her-name, can you tell her that I like her?" By then, I had become quite popular and pretty cool with many of the cute girls in school. I was The Boy.

As boys in the early adolescence stage, we are simply not mature or sophisticated enough to express and articulate our true feelings. Girls often misinterpret the hair pulling, spit-ball throwing and mean comments as forms of dislike. However, the underlying motivations behind these actions and similar ones are to gain the attention of a girl and have some form of communication with her.

The inability to communicate or express themselves properly, accompanied by undeveloped courting techniques, is part of the reason why boys pretend they don't like you when they actually do.

My contention therefore, as I've illustrated, is that the main reason boys will pretend they don't like you when they do, is that they are not willing to risk losing the camaraderie established amongst their peers. This cowardly characteristic prohibits them from taking a stance on what they truly believe in, especially if it goes against the grain or the norm of their social circle. They do not wish to deal with the consequences of independent thinking, which often result in ridicule and ostracism.

This fundamental approach can transfer into adulthood. Some men will continue the pattern of pretending they don't like a woman when they actually do. The reasoning is still supported by the original premises, but now in addition to the old-boys'-club and their peers, they have the added pressure of complying with societal standards. It's one thing to have the boys tease you when you're a kid but when society does so, that takes it to another level. "Society" determines and selects a series of characteristics and criteria that defines beauty. In this case, "Society" refers to the small percentage of gatekeepers; fashion editors; talent / model agents and designers who dictate what is socially acceptable. Also, I might add, it is damn near impossible to keep up with their ever-changing beauty trends. One minute they're telling you thin lips are in and the next minute, they're urging you to get Botox injections to make them fuller.

Women are not totally guilt-free and can also perpetuate the pretentious behavioral pattern that some men harbor. Instead of commending men on being in a loving relationship, I have actually witnessed numerous times when women observing a couple said "He is way too fine to be with her", or "He must really love her, cause she looks a hot mess." Well ladies, this is exactly why men pretend they don't like you when they do. Surely, a man may have no problem admitting he likes you and whispering sweet nothings in your ear, behind closed doors but publicly he may deny it and pretend he has no interest in you what-so-ever. You may very well be one of those women who falls outside the current standard of beauty and the man just doesn't want to deal with the ridicule that comes with dating that type of woman. Some men are just not strong enough to admit that this plus-size, bald-headed, hairy, one-legged, humpbacked woman is beautiful in his eyes and he likes her. It's a lot easier to pretend he doesn't.

CHAPTER 2

WHY DO BOYS SAY THEY WANT A

GOOD GIRL AND DON'T KNOW

HOW TO TREAT ONE?

Most men eventually want to end up with a
woman they can bring home to mother. Some men
even seek women who have traits similar to their
mother. We desire a woman who has the potential
to be a great wife and excellent mother; a woman
who is nurturing, loyal, loving, respectful and
intelligent. We want her to be a lady in the streets
but a streetwalker in bed. We want a woman who
knows how to stroke the male ego without being
patronizing. A woman who knows when to shut the

hell up and let us watch the game and, damn it, we want a woman who knows how to be submissive! Yes, I said the "S" word, because frankly, that's what a lot of men want. It doesn't matter how you choose to define a "Good girl", every man wants someone who is "Good" for them.

We can wait until our face turns blue, but as my fifth grade teacher would say, "It's time to wake up and smell the coffee."

Just because you want something, it does not mean you are responsible enough to have it. Just because you want something, it does not guarantee you will value it once you acquire it.

As a boy, I remember I would go shopping with my mother and every time we would pass by a toy store, I would lose my mind. I would beg and plead with her to allow me to go in and check out the latest toys. She would always remind me that I could look but she was not buying anything. OK deal; because once I was in, the plan was to activate my puppy eyes and begin an irresistible begging strategy. I had come across the ultimate toy once again. "Mommy, if you buy me this toy, I will be the best boy in the whole, wide world and you don't have to buy me anything anymore!" Usually, this didn't work but that day, I guess moms was in a good mood and she bought me exactly what I wanted. I was ecstatic and I couldn't wait to get home and start playing with my new toy. Well, in less than a 24 hour period, I had already totaled my toy and it was completely broken. I was upset and started to cry. I ran to my moms and I said, "This stupid toy doesn't work" and I asked her to buy me another one. She explained to me that the toy did work and I had broken it. "I am not going to buy you another one. You have to learn how to take better care of your toys". I was angry at first because my toy wasn't working, but the lesson she was trying to teach me did. I remember vowing that the next time I got a new toy, I would take better care of it. Also, the fact that she didn't replace it was an introduction to understanding value.

Now, let us apply this scenario to the question, "Why do boys say they want a good girl and don't know how to treat one?" What if my mother never scolded me about breaking my toy and nonchalantly replaced it. As an adult, I still might not have a clear comprehension of the importance of value and responsibility. Some men have never been taught how to properly treat a woman. As I came across other life lessons, I was better equipped because I had a reference point which allowed me to relate and soak in the information that was being conveyed. When an older guy told me never to hit a girl because they're not as physically strong as me and I could break them, I understood. I immediately thought about my favorite toy and how I felt when I broke it. Breaking my toy and losing it taught me how to be gentle. It taught me about limits and boundaries. I had an understanding of how hard I could play with my toy before it reached the point where it would break. I was fortunate to have a mother who taught me how to treat a woman and other essential life lessons. I was fortunate to have female friends who explained some of the expectations that women have. Although I had no immediate male figure in my household, I was lucky enough to cross paths with men who, as they would say, "dropped jewels" and "schooled" me. Unfortunately, some men don't have these opportunities and were not taught these essential life lessons. Aside from having no reference point, they have limited intellectual capacity and poor social skills, which can inhibit comprehension of some of the most important life lessons. In some cases, they are misguided, having been taught the wrong things. These men are lost, clueless and don't have any idea how to correctly treat a woman.

Ladies, you can not come into a relationship with the assumption that every man knows how to treat a woman. Although they may genuinely want a good girl, they may not have been trained or educated enough on how to actually treat one.

My suggestion is to treat your p#@sy, your love life and your future like you are a CEO who is running an empire.

Here are a few protocols you should incorporate when being approached by potential suitors. Next time a guy approaches you, immediately run a "Background Check". Ask him questions about where he was raised and what type of family structure and environment he came from. How old is he? Age can be an excellent indicator to determine what stage of life he is in currently. Younger guys are usually still in the dating phase, while older men, who have been around the block, may be more willing and ready to settle down. After you have thoroughly completed your background check, you can determine whether or not this candidate is worth interviewing. Never feel obligated or pressured to take things to the next level. As a woman, you have intuition. Learn to trust it! If you don't feel any chemistry, then it's better to move on rather than forcing it, because more than likely you'll regret it later. If you are satisfied with the information you have gathered thus far, then it's time to move on to the next level: the interview.

However, there is one crucial step before the interview that many women forget to implement. Many of my female friends are guilty of this as well. They believe that if you're a grown-ass man, you should already know how to treat a woman and it is not their responsibility or obligation to show you. In all fairness, men are not psychics and as a CEO, if you are currently seeking new employees, wouldn't it be wise to first post a "job description", so potential candidates know exactly what they're applying for? In addition, it will also help you filter out unqualified candidates.

Ladies, do not forget to post a "job description" before you conduct an interview. You need to articulate and express exactly what you're looking for in a relationship. You need to post all of your requirements, desires and expectations. You have to be candid about your likes and dislikes. If you are looking for a multi-millionaire with a 10 inch penis who's a former Nobel peace prize recipient, then say so. This way, you don't have a man applying for a position with a GED when it requires a Ph.D. This is beneficial to both parties. It will save you both a lot of time and potential heartache. In addition to that, it is nearly impossible to generalize exactly how to treat a woman because it is subjective and based on individual preference.

Now that your suitor has a clear understanding of what the job requires, he has the option to dismiss or continue his pursuit. If he chooses to continue, then he is indeed stating that he has the necessary qualifications. It is still your job as CEO to find out if he actually does. This should be done during the interview process. Get to know your potential candidate by asking colorful, open ended questions. If you want to know his take on kids, don't ask him "Do you like kids?" because that could encourage a short or single-word answer. Instead, ask him, "What do you think are the best ways to keep children occupied when you're babysitting them?" Questioning in this manner encourages a fuller, more meaningful answer, in which he has to rely on both his feelings and prior knowledge.

If you are satisfied with the way he has handled the interview process, then it may be time to hire him and start dating. Remember, this is a new employee and it's an entry-level position. You still do not know this man well enough and he should remain on probation for a period of time. During this time, everything discussed during the interview process needs to transgress from speculative talk into actual action. He needs to prove that he is actually qualified for the position. Even if you feel he is doing well during the probation period, be mindful not to offer a raise or promotion too soon. This may diminish his incentive to grow and maximize his potential. Ladies, let me be frank; just because you're feeling this guy, don't be so quick to give him your heart or your p#@sy. The goal is to keep it intriguing and interesting enough where he has the desire to continue climbing up the ladder of love and eventually become your life partner. An intern or entry level employee does not become the partner of an empire overnight.

So why do boys say they want a good girl and don't know how to treat one? Remember, men can express whatever they want but it does not mean they are educated enough or responsible enough to handle what they desire. This reasoning is similar to why many countries impose a drinking or driving age requirement.

In addition, there is no guarantee that once

they acquire what they want, they will value it. Women should never stay in a relationship where men are treating them poorly because it sends the wrong message and they will never learn the value of treating a woman well. If my mother would have nonchalantly replaced my broken toy, the message would be loud and clear; there are no consequences, even when you mistreat your things. Well, if you don't know how to treat a woman, then the consequence should be that you don't get a good girl. That power remains with women. A man can only mistreat you if you allow it. One of the ways you can prevent this is to act as if you're a CEO running an empire and treat your potential suitors like new employees. Post a crystal clear job description of exactly what you're looking for in a relationship and how you expect to be treated. This can help you filter out unqualified candidates. Conduct a background check and thorough interview. If you decide to hire and start dating, remember to implement a probation period. Eventually, the goal is to end up with a life partner. Remember, you're in charge. If he wants a good girl and doesn't know how to treat one, as a CEO you can take time out to retrain him or at any moment, you can always fire him!

CHAPTER 3

WHY DO BOYS LIKE BIMBOS?

First let's take a look at the word "bimbo". "Bimbo" is an English term, generally used to describe a woman who is physically attractive but has a low intelligence. The term also refers to a woman who acts in a sexually promiscuous manner. It is often associated with the stereotypes of the "Dumb blonde" or "Party girl", or in the urban community, the "Jump off" or "Freak".

There are a number of reasons why men like

bimbos. Let us begin with the obvious. Bimbos are usually physically attractive. Men tend to place a higher priority on visual sexual stimulation than women. Women usually respond more to sensual touch, emotional or mental stimuli. Perhaps this is one of the main reasons why women don't generally purchase magazines portraying naked men or frequent female strip clubs. In fact, according to Nielsen/Net ratings and other reliable sources, only 1-in-3 visitors to adult entertainment sites are women. On the other hand, men were the main consumers responsible for thrusting the global adult industry sales to an estimated 97 billion dollars at one point. Forrester research also reported that 46% of the men who participated in adult entertainment activities were married. So while you're walking down the street criticizing a bimbo for showing too

much cleavage or wearing a micro mini skirt so

short that you can see the color of her panties--if

she's wearing any--your husband or boyfriend may

appear to agree with your position but truthfully,

more than likely, he's thinking, "She may be a

bimbo but she's a bimbo with a great pair of tits".

Secondly, our competitive nature has a lot to

do with why boys like bimbos. The bimbo in

popular culture has become symbolic as being the

ultimate catch or prize. Successful men are often

seen parading around with their bimbos or as some

would refer to them, "trophy wives". Besides

being physically attracted to the bimbo, many men

are attracted to them because they are perceived

as status symbols. They enjoy showing them off to their peers and competitors, as though they are owners of a show horse. "Look at my mare; look at how well groomed she is. I adorn her in diamonds and beautiful evening gowns. Her face is absolutely gorgeous and she has an hour glass figure that is impeccable." I have witnessed many men who have objectified women and only refer to them in a physical manner. The notion behind showing off their bimbo is to smoke the competition and to make them aware and envious of their achievements. To boastfully declare how successful and wealthy they've become! To pronounce that not only do I drive the best cars and live in the finest homes, I am also capable of acquiring the most beautiful women in the world, which in their superficial minds happens to be the bimbo.

Another reason why boys gravitate toward the bimbo is they are often seen as less of a challenge. In the courting process, a boy's objective is generally sexually and physically driven. When you're in this stage of your life, the goal is not to land a meaningful relationship. The goal is to score! The bimbo usually acts in a sexually promiscuous manner, which is cohesive to the goals of the boy. She dresses provocatively; is an exhibitionist and she is willing to participate in sexual activities more readily than women with higher moral standards. Parisian psychiatrist Ernest Charles Lasque in his 1877 classic article, "Les Exhibitonistes," described it as a sexual disorder and someone with a mental state that lies somewhere "between reason and madness".

The boy, on the other hand, looks at a woman with this type of behavior as fun, spontaneous and exciting. The woman with a heightened moral standard is viewed as too conservative or boring. The process of courting that type of woman takes too long; is way too challenging and too costly. These men don't have the patience or willingness to wait and get to know the woman better before they reach an intimate level. They want to skip the long conversations, flowers, dinners and cut to the chase. The bimbo and these type of men share a common ground because they're both only interested in having a "good time". Another reason why boys like bimbos is they feel more comfortable expressing their inner sexual perversions.

Many of the things that men are thinking or would like to say to a woman may be considered inappropriate or disrespectful.

For instance, if a complete stranger came up to you and said, "Nice rack, show me your tits," many women may be appalled. Contrarily, the bimbo welcomes this type of attention. She may view it as a compliment and respond with a shake of her breast or better yet, a flash. Many men absolutely love and fantasize about these type of women. One of the most notable American iconic figures is Hugh Hefner, founder of Playboy Enterprises. Hefner has undoubtedly successfully capitalized on the stereotypical image of the bimbo. Despite the fact that he is well into his eighties, he still enjoys and continues to surround himself with these type of women.

Why do boys like bimbos? Well for one, they're physically attractive. The courting process with bimbos seems to be a lot less challenging. Many men feel more comfortable expressing their inner sexual perversions with bimbos. Bimbos share a common sexual ground with men. Bimbos love to show off their goods and boys enjoy seeing them. Boys don't want to spend a lot of time trying to score and luckily, bimbos seem to operate at a similar pace. Lastly, often times in society, the bimbo is viewed as the ultimate prize and status symbol.

CHAPTER 4

WHY DO BOYS FEEL INTIMIDATED BY

SUCCESSFUL WOMAN?

In many cultures, boys are traditionally raised in a manner where they must act as protector, provider, ultimate decision maker and overall king of the castle. There is an underlying pressure for boys to conform to these characteristics, because in society, these traits have become the precedent to what defines a real man.

Many women, including my close personal friends, have mentioned that one of the most attractive things about a man is his ability to provide security. Security can be broken down into four basic subcategories:

Physical Security: the ability to physically protect them from danger.

Intellectual Security: the ability to make logical decisions that will be in their best interest.

Emotional Security: the ability to provide an atmosphere that is trustworthy, supportive and loving. An environment where a woman feels comfortable exposing her vulnerabilities.

Financial Security: the ability to provide life's

basic necessities--such as food, clothes and shelter--consistently and comfortably. Men who are able to provide these necessities in a luxurious manner are often highly regarded.

So what happens to the man who does not fit into society's definition of a "Man" or is not able to provide a woman with security? This man usually lacks confidence. He becomes insecure; he is bitter, depressed and often stressed. He may choose to be asexual and not pursue any type of intimate relationship with women. Some men become so psychologically defeated they can develop erectile dysfunction. The reason I am mentioning these traits is to clarify which types of men are usually intimidated by successful women.

Men who are equally or more successful and meet the necessary standards are generally not as intimidated. In fact, some are so confident; they may come off as arrogant or cocky. It is the insecure and unaccomplished man that is most likely to be intimidated because he believes he does not meet the required standards and has little to offer a woman. In his mind, he doesn't stand a chance at getting a woman of such caliber and deems her to be way out of his league.

Successful woman can present an alternative structure which challenges traditional male roles and redefines manhood. As more women entered the workforce, they became increasingly more independent. Advanced careers with high paying salaries helped to fuel the economic empowerment of women. This new found sense of independence and economic strength caused a cultural shift. Women who were traditional care-givers were now bread-winners. Traditional family structures evolved into modern day matriarchal structures. Terms such as stay-at-home-dad and "househusband" began to emerge. Many of the traditionally male gender roles were being replaced by women. This shift can be exceptionally intimidating to men, especially when the belief is that a successful woman will effeminate them and force them to conform to traditionally feminine roles.

Successful women were often heard saying, "I'm independent. I make my own money and

I don't need a man. Men are only good for one thing!" Basically, these women were reducing the role and contribution of men down to an erection. Many men felt as though successful women were too independent and didn't need them. They also believed that the underlying tone of these women was degrading and disrespectful.

A friend of mine always spoke about his desire to date a successful woman. After many failed attempts, he finally landed one. In the beginning, he bragged about how he was enjoying all the finer things in life. He constantly reminded us everyday how he rolled around town in a luxury car and spent nights at her lavish, high-rise condominium. As things progressed, she eventually asked him to move in with her. One night, the two of them got into an argument. Let's just say she immediately reminded him that his name was not on the lease and that he did not pay any bills. She suggested he pack his things and leave. He called me when the incident occurred and while I remember him being angry, I think he was more shocked and hurt at how disposable he was in her eyes. After all, it was only their first argument and she was already kicking him out.

Anyway, the two of them managed to work out their differences and decided that it was best to continue on with their relationship. It was her birthday and my friend invited everyone to go out and have a good time. We went to a nightclub and afterwards, headed to a 24 hour restaurant. Everyone was enjoying themselves; talking about how much fun they had dancing. Everything was fine. It was getting late and we all decided to call it a night. We asked for the check and the waiter returned, coincidentally placing the bill in front of my friend. Apparently, the two of them had agreed to some secret arrangement because it appeared as if he was signaling her under the table. She opened her clutch purse, handed him her credit card and all hell broke loose! At first, I couldn't understand why he was so upset. He just yelled, "Wow, you're really trying to embarrass me in front of everybody! Real nice! Real f#@king nice!"

Unlike their first incident, where I do believe

she was guilty of throwing her weight around and flaunting her success in his face, this time I didn't sense any malicious intent. She was pretty much caught up in talking about the festivities and she forgot to discreetly hand him her credit card. She was comfortable with the arrangement but apparently, he was not. Needless to say, that was the end of their relationship.

When I spoke to him about his relationship with her, he actually disclosed some pretty interesting things. One was the way people perceived him and the stereotypes that came along with dating a successful woman. Although she was the one who actually proposed the arrangement, her close friends still labeled him as a "user". In his relationship, the traditional gender roles were reversed and it emasculated him in society. Although more women are choosing this type of relationship, it is still not culturally accepted. He believed that being with a successful woman in that manner gave her too much ammunition. It didn't matter if it was intentional or not; he felt like he was always in a vulnerable position, waiting for his manhood to be attacked. That, in fact, was the most intimidating thing about dating a successful woman.

CHAPTER 5

WHY DO BOYS LIE?

Boys lie for just about everything. They lie about
how much money they make. They lie about their
"size". They lie about having a wife and kids. They
seem to lie about everything that lies under the
sun. The question is why? Why not be honest and
forthright? Are you crazy?

**Most men would rather choose castration over
truth.**

There is a secret solemn affirmation amongst men that says: Take it to the grave and in the event that you are caught, never confess, even if there is an overwhelming amount of evidence against you. In this chapter, we will break the code and reveal a few reasons behind the lie.

As I mentioned in the previous chapter, there is a societal standard that defines a "Man" and his role. Many men attempt to conform and live up to the standards but not all are successful. Those men who fall short naturally become more insecure. They develop strategies to conceal their insecurities and vulnerabilities. The common weapon of choice is the lie. Almost instinctively, men will shoot out lies more rapidly than a machine gun in order to keep their insecurities covered.

I asked this beautiful young lady on a date when I was a teenager and, to my surprise, she said, "Sure I would love to. We can catch a movie or something. By the way, do you drive?"

Immediately, I felt as though I was going into cardiac arrest, because I did know how to drive but I didn't have a car at the time. So technically, I could have answered "Yes" but I think we all know what she meant. So of course, I blurted out, "Yeah I drive".

I don't know what came over me. All I knew was that I wasn't going to miss out on this opportunity.

We exchanged numbers and she said I could pick her up on Friday at her house, at around eight. One problem: It was Thursday and that meant I had less than 24 hours to come up with a master plan. I was pacing back and forth. Time was winding down and I was still drawing a blank. Then it hit me; I did have one older friend with a car and maybe he'd donate his vehicle in the name of a young man coming-of-age and trying to go out with a hot girl. I asked him. He thought about it. Reluctantly and cautiously, he said "Yes", but jokingly warned me not to crash his car, because he really didn't want to hurt anyone. I didn't pay his threats much attention. I was so relieved. I could actually make my date, and might I say, it turned out pretty awesome!

Unfortunately, this put me in a position where I had to tell the truth or continue the lie. So after our first date, I told her that I was having car trouble and my car was in the repair shop. Even though I didn't have "my car", we continued dating. Everything was pretty smooth. However, on a later occasion, out of the clear blue sky, she turned to me and asked me about it.

"Hey, whatever happened to your car?" she asked. "I only got to drive in it once."

"Oh, that piece of junk!" I replied. "I am so mad! After sitting in the shop for 2 weeks, they tell me it can't be fixed and I should probably look into buying a new one. But baby, I wasn't planning on buying another car and honestly right now, I can't afford it. (Sigh!) This really sucks!"

To that young lady; first of all, thanks for being so understanding and consoling me. But ummm ... if you ever bump into this book, I just wanted to publicly tell you that I apologize for lying to you.

So why did I lie? Why did I go through all that trouble? When she first asked, why didn't I just tell her the truth? "I don't have a car and I don't know when I'll be getting one and, by the way, I feel like a loser but I still would like to take you out on a date."

Well, the truth is, I was trying to conceal my

insecurities. In my case, it was not having a car. All the cool guys had cars and I didn't. I was embarrassed and because I was insecure, I lacked the confidence to share the true me.

Another reason why men lie is not only to conceal their insecurities but to actually conceal their skeletons. If a man feels there is something in his past or present that will hinder his chances of being with you, there is a great chance that he will not reveal it to you. There are certainly a vast variety of examples but here are a few common skeletons that men try to keep to themselves:

He may lie about having a girlfriend or even worse, having a wife. This goes back to the old proverb of a man trying to have his cake and eat it too.

He may lie about having a STD.

He may lie about being incarcerated and having a criminal record.

He may lie about the number of kids he actually has, especially if they're by different women.

These are just a few samples. What ever it may be, he is usually lying about something that is more likely to be a liability rather than an asset to your life.

Then you have the habitual liar. This is a man who

tells lies frequently. He doesn't really have a motive or necessarily need a reason to lie. He enjoys telling false stories. He tends to exaggerate a lot. He is generally not a good liar. He's often very sloppy and does not focus on covering his tracks. He is the type of man to have a dead cell phone make the ringer sound with his mouth and answer the call "Hey, President Obama. I have to call you back. I am actually on a date right now." Habitual liars can be quite comical because of how easy it is to detect their lies. The habitual liar will say just about anything for attention.

The "delusional liar", as I like to call them, is a man that may have started off as a habitual liar but has crossed the line to the point where he starts to believe his own lies. He creates a separate identity and lives as a fictional character. He may choose to take on the role of someone he idolizes. It can be a character in a movie or a business mogul that he has read about. He literally thinks he is this person and tries to mimic that person's lifestyle. He even expects others to respond to him as such.

A close friend actually suffered from this. For recreational fun, he would play video games and would virtually live out his fantasies. In one of the games, he had become a crime boss with loads of money. He was the owner of a string of casinos and night clubs, as well as the leader of a small army. As he excelled in the game, his personality began to change in real life. He started calling himself a "boss". Now mind you, this guy lived at home with his momma and had no money at all. Yet he would approach women and when he did, he would tell them "Yeah I am an entrepreneur and I own a couple of casinos." His fake Rolex and polyester suit did not persuade them at all. When he didn't get the response he was looking for, he would get up and proclaim that it was their loss, because they did not know who he was.

Finally, one day, I had to slap him with a reality check and I told him, "Fool, you don't really own a flock of casinos! That's why the women are not responding to you like a boss!" Unfortunately and disturbingly, it was too late. He no longer could differentiate the virtual world of video games from the real world. It was sad to watch my friend lose himself and lose touch with reality. Obviously, he could not live up to the grandiose lifestyle that he created within his head. Eventually, reality did catch up with him and he became extremely depressed. The delusional liar is a man with serious psychological issues and should seek professional help.

The "opportunistic liar" is a professional liar. He is charming and cunning. His approach to lying is extremely calculated. He has little regard for principles or consequences. His main objective is to take advantage of any opportunity that arises. It may be as simple as trying to get you to sleep with him or it might be a more complex scheme in which he is trying to extract money from a wealthy widow or marry into a wealthy family. The opportunistic liar will say whatever it takes to get what he wants.

The opportunistic liar studies his subject extensively and conducts the necessary research to lower the resistance of the subject. If you're a doctor, he will study the medical journal and discuss current medical issues with you to make you think he has a genuine interest in medicine. If he overhears you telling your girlfriend that you love a man who wears Italian suits, the next time you see him, he'll make sure you see him in an Italian suit. If you like museums, he may secretly follow you and "coincidently" bump into you at the museum, in an attempt to deceive you into thinking that he shares a personal interest in the arts. The opportunistic liar will go to great lengths to nurture his lie. It is very difficult to detect his lies because he is such a skillful liar.

If there is such a thing as an honorable liar, it would have to be the man who chooses to lie to a woman because he doesn't want to hurt her feelings.

A lot of men believe that it is not worth telling the truth at the expense of hurting a loved one. If a wife cooks a lovely meal for her husband on their anniversary, the truth may be that the meal is the worst thing he ever tasted in his life! Maybe his wife couldn't cook if her life depended on it. If it were me and she were to ask, "Did you enjoy the meal?" I would definitely lie to her and say "Yes, absolutely!", because telling her the truth at this particular time would ruin the moment. I rather appreciate the fact that my wife was thoughtful enough to cook for me, than focus on how bad the meal tasted. Eventually, later on, I would tell her the truth in a loving manner, because I definitely wouldn't want to repeat having to eat another hot mess meal. I might suggest that we take some cooking classes together to help us learn how to cook each other's favorite meals. Although I do not support or justify lying, this is one scenario where I would tell a "Love Lie"

So why do boys lie? Some lie to conceal their

insecurities or their skeletons. Some are just
habitual liars. Some have psychological issues and
have become "delusional liars". Some men are
"opportunistic liars" and some men lie because they
love you.

CHAPTER 6

WHY DO BOYS CHEAT?

As the sun begins to set, he begins his ritual. He

yearns and longs for what is to come. The look

in his eyes is intense and if it was not for his own

reflection, he too would be afraid. He steps out

into the concrete jungle with an irresistible scent

of attraction. His attire camouflages him in the

night. His movements are swift yet stealthy. They

will never see him coming but they will all feel his

presence. He lurks and within minutes, he finds

his prey. She is beautiful and her curvaceous body

sends him into an animalistic rage. He attacks! At first she tries to resist but each bite of seduction weakens her. She gives in to him. She allows him to feed off her body until his belly is full. Still, this is not enough to either satisfy or quench his thirst for lust. He must hunt again.

Sounds like a scene straight out of a romance thriller doesn't it? Well if this were an actual casting call, there would be a long line of hopeful men auditioning for the lead role. One of the reasons why men cheat is because they are obsessed with the chase and addicted to the hunt. The thrill of conquering a new woman is intriguing and overwhelmingly stimulating. The problem is that once these men capture a woman, the thrill is gone

and they will leave her on the side of the road like a
dead carcass that has been striped to the bone.

Do not misinterpret a man's physical presence

as being present in the relationship. A man

can continue to be physical with a woman but

mentally and emotionally he has already ended

the relationship and has already moved on.

In men's locker rooms, I've overheard men saying
numerous times, "The only thing better than p#@
sy is new p#@sy!" This is a powerful statement. It
shows us that these type of men are never satisfied.
Even when they're in a great relationship, they
are willing to risk it all for the opportunity to hunt
and conquer new women. While the conquering

and actually getting the "p#@sy" is rewarding, the thrill lies in constantly chasing and hunting. These men are habitual cheaters and even if they agree to a monogamous relationship, they are not cable of commitment because they are polyamorous at heart.

Another reason why men cheat is because they want physical variety. These men believe no one woman can posses all of the physical attributes they are attracted too. Some men can be very fickle when it comes to what they desire. One minute a man is chasing after a woman with DD's, but when he gets her, he becomes bored with the DD's and wants a women with an A cup. One minute he likes blondes, the next he likes brunettes. It's absolutely fine to be attracted to all types of women. The issue is that he has unrealistic desires. No one woman can have a big butt and a small butt simultaneously or be 100% black and 100% white. So instead of making a commitment to one specific type, he opts to date different women at the same time in an attempt to collectively satisfy all of his physical desires. He has his white girl on Monday; his black girl on Tuesday; his big boob girl on Wednesday; his small boob girl on Thursday and so on and so forth.

Realistically, although a man is in a committed relationship, he will be attracted to other women. There is no crime in that. The crime is when you act on that attraction. So another reason why men cheat is they lack the discipline to stay committed. They don't know when to turn off the valve that can cultivate a new love interest. For example, your man has a female co-worker who is drop-dead gorgeous. He still has functional eyes, so of course, he recognizes this. Just your luck, she finds him attractive and begins to flirt with him. He starts off strong and lets her know that he is married or has a girlfriend. She says "Fine no problem. We can still be friends," and reassures him that there is no harm in two co-workers having lunch occasionally.

This is where a lot of men fail! They make the fatal mistake of not closing the valve when the pressure is low. Instead, they leave the valve open and let the pressure build up. When you're in a committed relationship, there is no need to get closer or be in intimate settings with anyone else besides your partner. It is pointless and the outcome is usually negative. However, these men will convince themselves that it's just harmless flirting and they have the ability to close the valve at any moment if necessary. Oftentimes, they overestimate their capabilities and before they know it, the pressure has built up and an overflow has occurred more rapidly than anticipated. Granted, many of them do not start out with the intentions to commit acts of infidelity but unfortunately, due to their lack of discipline, many men will regretfully find themselves beyond the point of no return. It is unavoidable. They must learn to develop the necessary discipline it takes to resist temptations. There is no magical solution. The only way to resist temptations is to resist it! In other words, if you don't want to risk drowning, then stay clear of the water.

Undoubtedly, "Why do boys cheat?" is perhaps the most popular issue that women have with men. Many of my female friends, at some point, have asked me this question and the majority of women I surveyed seemed to place this high on their list. Most responded in disbelief. They couldn't figure out why a man would cheat, especially if he has everything he needs. "I am a good woman. I am pretty. I am a great wife. Whatever he asks of me, he usually gets, so what's the problem? Why would he cheat on me?" Sorry ladies but I am going to have to burst your bubble. That's *your* perception of yourself, not your man's. The reason your man is cheating is that you're not his dream girl, and

he settled for you. Actually, you're not doing

everything he wants, so he cheats to fill a void. Take

a moment and let that marinate.

In the beginning of the relationship, when

you're first getting to know each other, you may

have discussed each other's likes and dislikes in

order to get a better feel for one another. During

these discussions, he might have mentioned one

or more of his personal desires which you might

have unawarely dismissed. For example, you guys

are talking about what you like sexually and he

says to you "I love it when a woman puts ranch

dressing between my toes and licks it off. If your

first reaction was, "Oh, hell no! What kind of crazy,

nasty crap are you into?" He might laugh it off but he'll make a mental note. If a pattern of rejections or incompatibilities continues, he might begin to close up and no longer share his deep personal desires with you because you are not providing a comfortable environment in which he can do so. At the same time, he realizes through the course of discussions that you guys do have a lot in common. So he compromises and suppresses his desires and moves forward with the relationship. Keep in mind the desires are only suppressed, not gone. At any moment, these desires can be triggered and reactivated and under the right circumstances, he will most likely jump at the opportunity or chance to fulfill his true desires.

The bottom line is; most men cheat because they

are trying to fill a void in their current relationship. Women make assumptions and often misinterpret the void. A number of women have pointed out that in addition to the cheating, it is extremely frustrating to find out their man has cheated on them with a less attractive woman. Well, this is assuming that looks are even a factor. He may cheat on you with a less attractive woman because she compliments him and caters to his ego. The void here is a need for his ego to be massaged, so in this particular case, how attractive you are doesn't really matter. On the flip side, let me give you an example where the void *was* looks.

A friend and I were both working on a music tour. We were constantly surrounded by beautiful video models and dancers. My friend and co-worker was married at the time. When he spoke of his wife, you could tell that he loved her and truly adored her. He described her as his best friend; a really cool girl, who had a lot of substance. At one of the rehearsals, we spotted this model that was absolutely beautiful. She had an exotic look and an amazing figure.

He tapped me on my shoulder and said to me, "Hey, did you see that girl? Damn! She is fine! Can you imagine waking up to that every morning? Now that's what I'm talking about! Must be nice... must be nice! I know I'm married but at least I can look!" This was followed by a nervous laugh, as he regained his composure and realized that his wife might not take kind to some of his remarks.

The one thing that stood out to me was when he spoke of his wife, he did that with admiration but when he spoke about the video model, he did that with passion.

The more we spoke, the more I realized that his wife was not his dream girl. He confessed that the video girls were more his type but he felt they lacked substance. His wife, on the other hand, had substance but was average looking. He eventually cheated on his wife with one of the video models because, in this case, the void was looks. At that moment, I had an epiphany.

There is a difference between compromise and

settling. Do not settle!

His marriage was destined for failure from the very beginning. He was never 100 percent attracted to his wife and quite frankly, she was not his ideal type. His ideal woman was beauty and brains. What he really wanted was a doctor who looked like a video model. That type of woman might be rare but she does exist. Realistically, there is no perfect woman. However, I do believe you can find someone who is perfect for you.

My suggestion for both genders is to make a list of the ten top things that you're looking for in a relationship or a mate. Place them in chronological order; one being the most valuable and ten being the least. One through five are the most valuable

qualities that you cannot live without. Five through

ten are qualities that you would like to have but are

willing to compromise. Here is an example:

Settling /non negotiable qualities

1. Intelligent and logical

2. Physically attractive, beautiful face, great

   body

3. Religious/Spiritual

4. High sex drive

5. Nurturing (must want to have children)

Compromise/negotiable qualities

6. Funny

7. Domestic- Cook/Clean etc.

8. Wealthy

9. Submissive

10. Good communicator

Qualities that fall between six and ten are negotiable. However, if you compromise any of your top priorities (one through five) that's not compromise; that's settling. Never compromise qualities you can't live without! If you do this, all you're doing is temporarily suppressing your true desires and as I have illustrated, anything can trigger and resurface them.

You will find yourself trying to have your cake and eat it too. However, if you don't settle and marry your dream girl or dream guy, you will have your cake with the icing on top.

It doesn't matter if it's an addiction to the hunt; a desire for variety, or an attempt to fill a void. Having a better understanding of why boys cheat still doesn't take away the pain it causes.

CHAPTER 7

WHY DO BOYS HIT GIRLS?

- One in every four women will experience domestic violence in their lifetime.

- 85% of domestic violence victims are women.

- Nearly half of the cases of domestic violence are never reported to the police.

This is according to the National Violence Against Women survey, the Bureau of Justice Statistics and other reliable sources. There is a misconception that domestic violence only refers to acts of violence within a marriage. However, it includes any act of violence or abusive behavior that occurs in an intimate relationship, such as dating; cohabitation; boyfriend; friend or family. Certainly, assault and battery can happen with a complete stranger but the term domestic violence or dispute generally refers to a case where the victim has a relationship and knows the attacker.

So why do boys hit girls? Well, if you ask some men, they will tell you "Don't blame me! Blame society!" Historically, women were considered to be the property of men and subordinates. Religious institutions, as well as judicial systems, have both at some point justified hitting women.

In the Qur'an, which is the central religious text of Islam, there is a highly debatable verse that appears to support the beating of women. In chapter 4, verse 34, the English translation by Abdullah Yusuf Ali: 1934 states:

004.034 Men are the protectors and maintainers of women, because God has given the one more (strength) than the other, and because they support them from their means. Therefore the righteous women are devoutly obedient, and guard in (the husband's) absence what God would have them guard. As to those women on whose part ye fear disloyalty and ill-conduct, admonish them (first), (Next), refuse to share their beds, (And last) beat them (lightly); but if they return to obedience, seek not against them means (of annoyance): For God is Most High, Great (above you all).

Muslim scholars argue that this text is often taken out of context and does not advocate domestic abuse or violence. However, it does allow a husband, as a last resort, to use light physical force in order to protect and maintain obedience with his wife.

In the United States, there was a case in North Carolina where a man was indicted for beating his wife and found not guilty.

State v. Rhodes

61 N.C. 453 (1868)

The defendant was indicted for an assault and battery upon his wife, Elizabeth Rhodes. Upon the evidence submitted to them, the jury returned the following special verdict:

"We find that the defendant struck Elizabeth Rhode, his wife, three licks with a switch about the size of one of his finger (but not as large as a man's thumb), without any provocation except some words uttered by her and not recollected by the witness."

His Honor was of the opinion that the defendant

had a right to whip his wife with a switch no larger than his thumb, and upon the facts found in the special verdict, he was not guilty in law. Judgment in favor of the Defendant was accordingly entered and the State appealed.

The State Supreme Court eventually repudiated the argument but dismissed the case on the basis that the husband did not actually substantially harm his wife. Therefore, the rule of thumb was illegal but the courts decision of dismissal indirectly implied that it was perfectly legal to beat your wife as long as you didn't inflict severe damage.

Our society certainly derives from a patriarchal system which, at one point, allowed men to legally chastise their wives. We no longer live under such a system and it does not matter if you beat your wife lightly or use a switch smaller than a man's thumb. Any unwanted physical contact is a crime, legally and morally.

Although times have changed, there are still many men who choose to hold onto ancient philosophies. They still regard women as property, subordinates and servants. This mentality makes it that more comfortable for them to strike women. There is no sound reason as to why boys hit girls. These men simply have no respect for women. I have discussed this subject with men and often, I am appalled by the position that some of these men take. One dude actually told me, "Sometimes you have to check a b*tch if she doesn't know her place!" Another one said, "If a woman provokes a confrontation and wants to act like a man, then she deserves to be treated like one." Some men had the audacity to compare adult women to children. They believed in the same manner that a parent spanks their child, a women should also be spanked if she does something wrong. It is quite obvious that these type of men do not see women as equal peers.

While these men have no respect for women, they command respect *from* them. They claim that they only hit women when they are being utterly disrespectful. I witnessed an argument between a friend of mine and his girlfriend. He told her to get in the car and go home because he didn't want to argue in public. Well, she took offense and said,

"Don't tell me what to do! If I want to yell I will

yell!" She then proceeded to announce all the things

that made him less of a man. One of the things

she mentioned was that he had a small penis that

didn't work and she was totally clueless as to why

she even dated him for so long. She went on to call

him a "broke bum" and made everyone aware that

the car he was driving was actually hers. The last

couple of statements clearly pushed him over the

edge, because without warning, he slapped her right

in the face!

I remember feeling like the world had stopped.

I was stunned! I couldn't believe my friend was

capable of hitting a woman. I jumped in and

separated them and I looked him straight in his eye and I said, "Not in front of me!" At the time, that was all that came out but what I meant to say was there was no way in hell I was going to allow him to beat a woman in front of me. Regardless, he understood exactly what I meant and he backed off. We spoke afterward and he told me never in his life had he hit a woman before and it was actually the first time he'd ever done anything like that.

He kept saying, "She kept pushing and pushing and I couldn't take it no more! Did you hear the way she was talking to me?"

"Yes," I said, and told him I agreed that much of the things she said were disrespectful and perhaps she was hitting below the belt. However, it was still

no justification to resort to violence. My friend and

a lot of men have no self control. They are poorly

skilled at anger management and conflict control.

Another incident I witnessed was not exactly

a domestic dispute. This dispute occurred while

attending a party. There was a gentleman who was

trying to talk to a young lady. The young lady did

not like his approach and immediately went on a

rant. She talked about everything possible from his

ugly face to his beat up shoes. She gave him every

reason why she would never give him the time of

day. The crowd enjoyed the antics but shortly after,

things began to escalate and turn for the worst.

Her comical approach turned into rage. She started

yelling and putting her hands in his face.

He said, "If you don't move your f#@king hands out of my face, I will smack the sh*t out of you!"

This did nothing but enrage her even more and she dared him to do it. "I wish you would put your hands on me! I wish you would!"

Well, he didn't actually put his hands on her. He decided to hit her across the head with a champagne bottle. The entire club was in disbelief. The young lady who was quite boisterous now stood there silently, holding her head, with tears running down her eyes.

Why do boys hit girls? Well some boys can't handle disrespect, embarrassment or rejection. They deal with these issues in an uncivilized manner, as if they were prehistoric troglodytes. Ladies, it is always in your best interest to be non-confrontational, especially with strangers, because you never know what type of man you're dealing with.

In the nightclub incident, I actually overheard both women and men saying that the guy was intoxicated and perhaps this was the reason why he struck the girl with the bottle. Well, alcohol does not cause battery, nor does any other substance abuse cause it. Certainly, there is a high correlation between the two but it is not a causal relationship.

A batterer may be an alcoholic or drug addict.

Often they will use substance abuse as an excuse

to place the blame and responsibility of their

violence elsewhere. Alcoholism and battering are

overlapping yet independent problems and should

be addressed separately.

In fact, many of the men I encountered used

alcohol and other substances as a way to self

medicate and cope with more deeply rooted issues.

Many of them suffered from depression, suicidal

thoughts, chemical imbalances and other forms of

mental illness. Not being able to cope with their

issues is more likely why these men choose to act

out violently. In most cases, what the woman said

or did was trivial. These men were more frustrated

with themselves.

These men are cowards who prey on the weak. It is a known fact that men are generally physically stronger than women. These men take advantage of this and they feel comfortable attacking a woman because they don't see women as a threat or as someone able to competently defend themselves. Their goal is to weaken a woman in every aspect; physically, mentally and emotionally. For instance:

Women who are economically dependent are less likely to leave an abuser because they have no money and nowhere to go. Mentally, they are less likely to devise an escape strategy and seek help because emotionally, they feel hopeless.

Why do boys hit girls? Ultimately, it's a tactic used to intimidate and dominate; to gain total power and control. These type of men choose to be dictators rather than leaders. They resort to using force because they lack intelligence, charm and persuasive communication techniques. Batterers come in all forms, regardless of educational level; income level; race; religion or profession. Some men blame society and how they were raised. Well, there might be some validity to that point. According to the National Coalition Against Domestic Violence, boys who witnessed domestic violence are twice as likely to abuse their own partners and children when they become adults. Other men blame alcohol and argue that they were provoked. Regardless of what outside entity you choose to use as an excuse, as a man, you must learn to have self control and take full responsibility for your actions. Opinions about hitting women will vary from country to country and era to era. In my neighborhood, it was simply put: "Real men don't hit girls".

CHAPTER 8

WHY DO BOYS RAPE?

Rape is defined as unlawful, forced or non-consensual sexual intrusion. Rape can be categorized in different ways. These are a few types of rape:

Stranger rape- enacted by someone unknown to the victim.

Acquaintance rape- committed by someone you know or have met. It is also known as date rape.

Marital rape- is when the perpetrator is the victim's spouse.

Gang rape- when a group of people participate in the rape of a single victim.

Statutory rape- when adults engage in sex with minors under the legal age of consent. This also includes sex with mentally challenged adults.

I must admit, I was totally naive to the amount of women who have been victims of rape. It wasn't until I spoke with my female friends that I realized a majority of them have either been raped, sexually assaulted or narrowly escaped being raped. Somewhere in America, a woman is raped every two minutes according to the U.S. Department of Justice.

As my friends continued to share their stories of rape, I became increasingly angered, especially after finding out that none of them had reported their attacks. My first reaction was "Why didn't you tell someone? Why didn't you call the police?" Their responses varied. Some felt ashamed and embarrassed. Some believed the rape was their fault. Some felt that even if they notified the authorities, enough wouldn't be done to protect them and all it would do is agitate their attacker, which would put them more in harms way. Others explained that they wanted to protect their family members and feared that if any of them found out, they would attempt to kill their attacker. They decided it was best the attack remain a secret, rather than risk their loved ones going to jail.

After sharing her story, one of my dear friends asked, in a soft vulnerable voice, "Why do boys rape?" I was torn and saddened and although I had never personally raped a woman, I was totally committed to providing my friend, as well as other women, with some insight on this issue.

Let's begin with my own personal story. I remember going to elementary school. I was in the 3rd grade. I was either seven or eight years old. I was amongst the trouble-makers and class clowns. I don't remember exactly how or who started this particular "game" as we called it. For a time period, a few of the guys in my class came up with the idea that we would pinch the girls' butts and run. Eventually, it escalated to a few seconds of dry humping. The girls in the class all responded differently. Some girls giggled and thought it was fun. Even when they made threats to tell the teacher, we all knew they were bluffing. However, there were those girls that did tell the teacher on us. There were a select few that gave us a look like, "Don't even think about it!", and if we did, they would attack us like wild hyenas.

There was one particular girl who was really cute. All the boys liked her. She was extremely quiet. A few of us, including myself, would squeeze her butt but unlike the other girls, she didn't giggle nor fight back. She had no response at all. For some reason, we focused on this girl and it became an everyday ritual. This went on for some time, because although some of the girls told on us, they never gave the teacher exact details. They only mentioned that we were bothering them. The teacher would tell us cut it out or place us in the corner for a few minutes, totally unaware of the severity of our actions.

One day, right before class started, the girl we all liked was about to sit down, so I came up with the brilliant idea that I would slide into her chair right before she sat down so she would end up sitting on my lap. It was a new innovative move and all the boys started laughing and even some of the other girls. I didn't think it was a big deal but then she started to cry. I immediately got up and I felt really bad. I liked her. I was horsing around but I did not want to make her cry. While I was feeling bad, some of my classmates just didn't grasp the concept of enough-is-enough. They kept pinching her butt. I became too scared to try anything anymore. I didn't want to get in trouble and it wasn't fun or funny now that I made her cry. One of the other boys did it again and finally she turned around and said, "Stop it, leave me alone!" She still didn't tell the teacher on us, so we all thought we were in the clear.

The next day, unannounced to us, the girl shows up with her father. I was thinking "I am only eight and my life is over! Boy, am I in big trouble!" Then she began to pick us out like criminal suspects, standing in a line-up. Her father had asked to talk to all of the boys involved and I was one of them. Before he could begin, I just started crying uncontrollably. I was scared out of my mind. Her father had a deep baritone voice but oddly he wasn't yelling or as angry as I anticipated. He spoke to us like we were his children as well. I remember exactly what he said.

"I know you guys are boys and you like the girls," he told us, "But you have to take it easy on the girls. They're delicate. My daughter comes home every day crying and I don't think you guys want to make her cry."

Her father was an amazing man, because during his speech, he even took time out to console me. He told us all that everything was going to be all right and assured us that he just wanted to talk, so there was no need for all the tears. He ended his stern speech with a question.

"You are all boys who are becoming young men and you have to protect and take care of the girls. Do you understand?"

With tears in my eyes and snot running from my nose, I timidly said, "Yes."

He then jokingly warned us not to make him come up to the school again, because the next time, he wouldn't be so nice. He smiled and placed his hand on my shoulder but it felt more like I was being embraced by a grizzly bear. Our principal, on the other hand, wasn't so calm and collected. He yelled at us, then sentenced all of us to weeks of detention.

What did I learn from this experience? Although we were just little boys who had no concept of what sexual assault or harassment was, we did know right from wrong. We knew squeezing girls' butts was wrong, because we only did it when the teacher wasn't looking. It's never too early to address these issues with your children. Don't just sweep it under the rug. I am forever thankful that I got in trouble and the girl's father came up to the school to speak with us.

He helped me to understand that you can't solely act on sexual impulses at the expense of hurting or violating someone else.

One of the other things I discovered was that even at eight years old, I had compassion way before her father came up to the school. I felt bad because our game was making a girl cry. Why did I feel compassion when some of the other boys didn't? They were completely comfortable with continuing on; despite her clearly displaying that she was uncomfortable. Another thing that I observed was that, even at that age, we knew to prey on the weak. The girls that fought back or told on us to the teacher, we didn't harass as much or at all. We turned our attention and focused on those girls that didn't mind us feeling them up or didn't tell on us when we did. Interestingly enough, even after we got in trouble, some of the boys still wanted to continue playing the game. I personally had been scared straight. I was still a curious boy and after I had gotten in trouble, I just thought it would be safer to ask the girls instead of pinching their butts without permission. I didn't completely stop, because I still had those sexual desires and they continued on into my adolescent and adult stages. Biologically, boys are sometimes flooded with hormones and are overwhelmed with sexual desires and impulses. As a teenager, I wanted to jump every girl because my hormones were going crazy and I was on a quest to fulfill many of my sexual curiosities. Even as a mature adult, there are still occasions were a woman can walk by wearing a sexy pair of heels, a low cut top or fitted dress and some crazy sexual impulsive thought enters my mind.

The issue is not having sexual desires or impulses. The issue is about not having sexual restraint.

Luckily for me, I learned the importance of restraint at eight years old. Why do boys rape? Because some still have not learned to restrain themselves from acting on their sexual desires or impulses.

We are no longer talking about a group of

preadolescent third graders. If this inappropriate behavior is not addressed early on, many boys will tend to carry it into their adult lives. I am sure many of you have witnessed or heard of men participating in inappropriate sexual activities at concerts and outdoor festivals, such as Spring break, Bike week or Mardi Gras. It may start off with a request to publicly show your boobs. Some women don't mind participating at this level but as the alcohol increases and more men become aware that women are baring their breast, the crowd usually tends to get more aggressive. It can often turn from a flash to being groped by dozens of out-of-control men.

Even when this type of behavior occurs, it is treated lightly. The women often try to get away when they are overwhelmed but again, many don't believe it's serious enough to report. Onlookers might be appalled but are not willing to report the inappropriate behavior to the authorities. Group sexual assault is often looked at as boys-being-boys but they're not boys; these are men, who are totally competent and aware of inappropriate behavior! One of the reasons why boys rape is because they feel that there are no real consequences. Victims will more than likely not report the attack.

The girl who does not tell the teacher becomes the woman who does not tell the police.

Not telling sends out the wrong message to these type of men. It tells them that, more than likely, they will face no consequences for their inappropriate behavior. It tells them that their behavior can't possibly be all that bad if a woman doesn't think it's worth reporting. Groping is often looked at as boys just having good old-fashioned fun.

Groping is not good old-fashioned fun. It's sexual assault. It is a gateway behavior that can lead to more violent sexual assaults like rape.

One of the most notable cases occurred on June 11, 2000, in New York City's Central Park, during and after the Puerto Rican Day parade. A group of men started out dousing women who passed by with water. Eventually, it led to pulling off women's clothes and sexually molesting them. It was reported that some women accused the group

of men of penetrating them vaginally with their

fingers and tongues. A few of the victims were also

minors. In addition to being sexually assaulted,

some victims were also robbed. In the beginning

of the attacks, it was still regarded as reckless fun.

Still, no reports were made. Some parade-goers

even started video-taping the assaults. The so-called

fun had turned into a violent, sexual, group-attack.

It was eventually reported to the police and even

then, it was met with indifference. The video tapes

of onlookers would eventually lead to 33 men being

arrested and more than half of them being found

guilty. Over 56 women reported being sexually

attacked that day. (*streetharrassmentproject.org*)

Taking you out to dinner, whispering sweet nothings in your ear or showering you with gifts are all things a wooer does when he is trying to win the heart of a woman.

Unfortunately most men are not trying to win hearts. They are trying to conquer vaginas.

The whole courtship process is viewed as tedious and unnecessary. These men are not interested in women who are too much of a challenge or have too many requirements. They're looking for the quick and easy way out. They want women who are weak, vulnerable and easily manipulated. Many men have come to the realization that mature women are not easily manipulated, so they have turned their focus on minors. These men prey on young women who are under the legal age of consent. They manipulate and coerce them into having sex. Engaging in sexual acts with a minor is considered statutory rape. Many of these men feel they have done nothing wrong, especially if the minor consents. However, the law still presumes coercion because the minor is not of the legal age where they are capable or competent to consent to sexual conduct. Sadly, this type of rape appears to be socially accepted amongst men. On numerous occasions, I have witnessed men openly confess to statutory rape or admit that if given the opportunity, they would take it.

I remember watching a football game with a

group of guys and the half-time show featured a fifteen year old singer. Guys started commenting about how they would "do her". One guy yelled out, "Hey, she might be young but her body is ripe and ready for the picking, man! I would f#@k the sh*t out of that little girl!" The majority of the guys laughed in agreement. I was just thinking, "Wow, how the hell can you lust after a little girl? Are you crazy?" The laughs and steady flow of derogatory comments that filled the room were a clear indication that I was outnumbered, and perhaps, the only one who felt a certain way.

Another friend, who happens to be in his late thirties, mentioned his affair with a minor. He said it in a manner almost as if he was proud of his rape.

He ranted, "Man, this chick is only 15 or 16 years old but man she knows how to f#@k! Damn, her p#@sy was so tight, it was like f#@king a virgin!"

Even an executive in upper level management pulled me to the side to tell me about his exciting trip abroad, in which he engaged in sex with minors. He made it a point to mention that they're not as uptight about sleeping with young girls over there. The purpose of being so candid is to illustrate how openly and socially accepted statutory rape has become within the male community.

Another tactic that men use to escape the courting process is to engage in drug facilitated rapes. This is the type of rape where a guy uses drugs or alcohol to impede their victim's judgment and to compromise their abilities to consent to sexual activities. Drugs and alcohol are also used to minimize the resistance and memory of the victim of sexual assault. Getting a girl tipsy or drunk to increase your chance of having sex with them is certainly a common practice amongst men. Countless times, I have overheard men huddled up and plotting, as if they were going over a winning game play. "OK, on three, we get the girls drunk, loosen them up and have sex! 1, 2, 3, Get Drunk!"

Going on a date and having a few drinks is normal but intentionally trying to get a girl drunk so that you can take advantage of her is not.

There was a drug facilitated rape which occurred on my college campus. Some of the more popular guys were video taping girls having sex. The tapes were leaked and eventually circulated around the entire campus dorm rooms. I remember watching one of the tapes and after a while, I realized I was actually watching a rape. One of the guys had gotten a girl so drunk that she was in-and-out of consciousness. You could see her mumbling, "What are you doing?" then shortly afterward, she would pass out. On the tape, she tried to push him off but she was so dazed and weak that her push looked more like a caress. All the while, this guy was on top of her, having sex. After he was done, he took off all her clothes and while she was still completely blacked out, he started fondling her and making silly faces at the camera. Eventually, word got back to the girl about the tape and she was furious! The ironic thing was all her girlfriends, whom by the way were also taped and happened to be dating friends of the attacker, convinced her not to tell the authorities. In fact, some stated that it was her own fault for allowing herself to get that drunk and they accused her of lying about not remembering anything. Basically, everyone on campus knew what happened but the incident, to my knowledge, was never reported.

Another incident happened with a good friend who invited me to a club in the city. We were having a good time, dancing and having a few drinks. He spotted this cute girl, walked over and began to converse with her. I saw them dancing and laughing and it looked like she was also attracted to him. At one point, I even saw them exchange numbers. I was off doing my own thing and I ended up leaving them by the bar area. Next thing I know, there was an eruption of confusion and a bunch of the club's bouncers started running over to the bar area. I turned to see what was happening and I saw my friend getting roughed-up by security. I headed over and all I kept thinking was "My boy was just having a drink with a young lady. Why in the hell are they treating him like this?" They literally threw him out of the club. I was pissed off and I still didn't know what happened.

I approached one of the bouncers aggressively, like "What the hell is going on? Why did you do that to my friend?"

He looked at me and said, "You know that guy? Well, we have cameras over by the bar area and we caught your buddy putting drugs in that girl's drink. We don't tolerate that crap here. Do you have a problem?"

I was speechless and in disbelief. I said, "I appreciate you kicking him out, because if he did that, he deserved that and more."

We shook hands and I went back to dance floor and continued partying. I had known that guy for over nine years and after that incident, I have not heard from him since. Interestingly enough, the girl he was trying to drug was already attracted to him. In addition to that, he happens to be a charming, good looking guy who never had a problem attracting women. However, he was impatient and refused to go through the whole courting process. He didn't want to go on a date. He wanted to sleep with her and he wanted to do it that night! In his mind, drugging her was the sure-fire way.

Another reason why boys rape is that some men are power-mad control-freaks who have a sense of entitlement. For example, these men, if they take you out on a date or buy you a gift, believe they are entitled to sex. Some men in powerful positions feel if they help a woman, they're entitled to some sort of sexual compensation. They say things like "If I do hire you, what are you going to do for me?" Some men are narcissistic. They feel because they are exceptionally talented or handsome or financially successful, they should be treated like royalty and are entitled to women servants; no exceptions to the rule.

I actually went to school with this type of guy. We were both on the basketball team. He was a star player and all the girls thought he was super fine. He had a lot of machismo and he was extremely athletic. At the time, he was being scouted by a few professional NBA teams. In his mind, it was his world and he was the greatest gift to women.

He openly dated multiple women at school and he openly disrespected them. He had little regard for their feelings. He always referred to women as b*tches.

Even when word got around that he was a complete jerk, his poor reputation still did not stop girls from flocking to him. I remember, after a game, one of the girls he was allegedly sleeping with said something to him and, in front of everyone, he said to her, "All I need you to do is keep sucking my d*@k and shut the f#@k up!" Up until this point, no one knew the exact details of their relationship and you could tell by the look on her face that she didn't want that information publicly disclosed. She was embarrassed and hurt.

He was very much into power and control and didn't have a problem flaunting it. In the locker room, he would boast that he could get any girl to do anything for him. He even offered to provide other team players with sexual favors from any girl of their choice. The way it worked was this: if a girl showed interest in him, he would tell her if she ever wanted a real chance to be with him, she was first required to have sex with one of his boys. It sounds crazy but a lot of girls were willing to subject themselves to this type of degradation. Even though he was incredibly disrespectful toward women, he still was not a rapist. At least that is what I thought at the time.

A couple of years after we graduated, I started

dating this girl. I really liked her and we had a pretty good connection but for some reason, every time we started to get intimate, she would push me away. It got to the point where she didn't want me to touch her at all. I was confused because she told me she wanted to but she couldn't. I asked her why countless times but she never gave me an answer. Being in a non-intimate relationship didn't bother me but knowing that somehow she was hurt and not knowing why, just killed me. One night we were just sitting there on her bed and she decided to open up to me. She told me that my physique reminded her of a guy that raped her. Since the incident she had not been in an intimate relationship, it was hard for her to feel safe when a man touched her, because her last memory was one in which she was violated.

She continued sharing her story. She said she really

didn't know the guy that well; they were on their

first date. They had only spoken a few times on

the phone prior to the date. After the date ended,

he asked her to come back to his place and chill.

She was hesitant but she went anyway. They

ended up kissing and making out. Then he tried to

take her jeans off. She stopped him and told him

that she was not ready to have sex with him. He

started violently yelling at her and claimed that

she knew why she was here and he accused her

of playing mind games. She pleaded with him to

stop but he did not listen. He threw her on the bed

and proceeded to rape her. She told me her body

went numb and all she remembered was crying and

waiting for it to be over. Her telling me this made

me cry. Although it happened over a year before we became involved, I became instantly angry because it felt like it was happening right before my eyes. I asked her to give me his information, because honestly, I wanted to beat his ass! She refused at first but eventually she told me his first name. It was like I was having an outer body experience immediately after she said his first name.

I said his last name and with immense conviction, I told her, "I know who raped you!"

She looked at me as if she saw a ghost. "Oh, my God! Yes, that is his last name. How did you know?"

It turned out that the guy who raped her was, in fact, my old basketball teammate. This is a classic example of what is referred to as date rape.

Another reason why boys rape is some men actually hate women. They have an animosity and a deep anger toward women. Their main goal is to punish and degrade women. These type of men are very impulsive and they have explosive tempers. They are the type of men who will randomly grab a victim and pull them into a nearby alley. They are not looking to kill you but they will beat you to near unconsciousness before committing the rape.

Some men rape because they are sadistic. These type of men get sexual gratification from inflicting pain or emotional abuse on others. These men are very charming and intelligent. The crime is usually premeditated and methodical. They usually seek to gain absolute control of their victims. They will tie, gag and blindfold their victims, then torture them over a period of days. This is the least common type of rape but the most violent. He usually kills his victims to either cover up evidence or satisfy some psychosexual need.

Another reason why some boys rape is they suffer from some sort of mental disorder. They are delusional and obsessive. This type of man lives near you or possibly he is a co-worker. He is not athletic and he lacks self confidence. He doesn't have good enough interpersonal skills to develop relationships with women. He is often addicted to pornography. He pre-selects his victim by peeping or stalking her. He fantasizes that he is the victim's lover. He may take photos of the victim without her knowledge. He typically breaks into her home in the early morning and awakens her. He may attempt to kiss the victim and engage in foreplay before committing the rape. He is the least violent type of rapist; he does not intend to kill or hurt his victim. (*Profile Of A Rapist, Paralumun.com*)

Recently there have been debates on whether or not to include "rape by deception" under the legal definition of rape. Sabbar Kashur, a 30-year-old Arab man was convicted of rape by deception after he had consensual sex with a woman who believed him to be a fellow Jew. In 2010, the Jerusalem district court sentenced Kashur to 18 months in prison and the court ruled he was guilty of rape by deception. One of the judges, Tzvi Segal, stated although not a "classical rape by force", the women would not have consented to sex if she had not believed Kashur was Jewish. Therefore, the sex was obtained under false pretenses. (*guardian.co.uk*)

Could a similar verdict occur in the United States? Well, there is one case that happened in Massachusetts where a man impersonated his twin brother and slept with his brother's girlfriend in the middle of the night. The sex was consensual and the court ruled that "intercourse where consent is achieved by fraud does not constitute rape". (*Could a pick up artist be charged with rape by deception,*

Ryan McCartney msnbc.com)

Massachusetts and several other states including
California, Tennessee and Alabama have all included
forms of rape by fraud into state legislation. Is this a
new motion toward redefining the traditional legal
definition of rape?

Regardless of how rape is defined or categorized,
the one thing that is consistent throughout is all types
of rape violate its victims. Unfortunately, there is no
sure way to prevent rape but hopefully, my experiences
and research have given my personal friends and other
women some insight on "Why do boys rape?"

CHAPTER 9

WHY DO BOYS CHOOSE NOT TO

COMMUNICATE?

When I first got approached with this question,

I was puzzled. What do you mean, boys don't

communicate? As women began to go into further

detail, I suddenly realized it's not that boys don't

communicate; we don't communicate the way

women want us to. I thought the best way to tackle

this issue was simply to address some of the popular

scenarios women asked about and point out the

forms of communication and reasoning behind it.

One of the most popular issues had to do with men who just stop calling or break-up without saying anything. Okay, you meet a guy and he clearly expresses interest. You guys exchange numbers and eventually start talking on the phone. In the beginning, you may have talked all night until the very next morning. Perhaps there is enough interest that you guys eventually start dating. This is the perfect time to press the pause button. Have you noticed that you're the one that always initiates the calls and he just responds to them? This is the first form of communication *if you're always calling.* He is communicating that he is not that intrigued by you. He is not that interested and he doesn't mind dealing with you but you're disposable. If you call, he will respond, but if you don't, it's not that big of a deal. Men will say, "Ugh, she's OK I guess if she throws the p#@sy at me, I'll take it."

I find that women sometimes are so over zealous about starting a new relationship that they often overlook this type of communication. It may turn from him only responding to your calls, to not responding at all. Yes, he may have been genuinely interested in you but now he realizes that he is not. Perhaps it was something you said or did that has completely turned him off. It doesn't matter whether it's a short term or a long term relationship.

When a guy stops calling, it is clear communication that he is no longer interested in you and he does not wish to discuss it. Period.

Women will go on to say it's rude or inconsiderate and feel they are owed some sort of explanation. Well, we're not talking about dating etiquette here. We're talking about communication, although you may not agree or like the way it was communicated. Regardless of how, it was in fact clearly communicated. Women may feel more comfortable with verbal communication but it's not the only form of communicating. Some men may communicate through facial expression or body language.

Some men may choose to communicate by not communicating at all.

"Why?" you might ask. As I have mentioned before, the man has communicated that he is not interested. It's not open for discussion, so calling you to explain why he is no longer interested is still a discussion. Some women have complained that men often send mixed signals. This is true but that fact that you feel like you're receiving mixed signals means that it was communicated. He says he likes you but he never shows it. He calls, and then he disappears, then pops up only when he wants something. You may have access to him when it comes to sex but if you need his support for other personal issues, he is no where to be found. He is clearly communicating that he is not willing to be consistent throughout the relationship. He is communicating that he is indecisive about how he truly feels about you. Sometimes he wants you and sometimes he doesn't. Most women recognize the inconsistent pattern but often opt to ignore or overlook it in the name of love.

Another reason men don't verbally communicate is they don't want to hurt your feelings and be responsible for pointing out your flaws. Yes, you may be hurt by him not calling you but the reason behind it is still a mystery. For example, I was dating a woman and it was on the very night that we were supposed to be intimate for the first time. Every thing was perfect. She came out of the shower and she looked amazing. I couldn't wait to tear her up and as I got to embrace her, I noticed that her vagina smelt like wet garbage. Well, that certainly ruined the mood. I was not about to have

a discussion about hygiene. If a woman comes

out of the shower smelling like wet garbage,

that is something they need to discuss with their

gynecologist, not their date. A horny man bolting

out the door and leaving you while you're half

naked is enough communication that something

is terribly wrong. Sometimes a man just doesn't

want to deal with a potentially messy, hurtful or

confrontational situation and prefers to make a

clean break.

Another concern that women had was in the

bedroom. Some women pointed out that their mates

are not expressive and don't communicate how

they feel sexually. So they have no clue if they're

pleasing them or if they're doing a particular act right. I am going to keep this simple. If your man is not telling you to stop, then it's fine and it's safe to assume he likes it. I am pretty sure if you do something he doesn't like and can't tolerate, he will certainly let you know in some shape or form. Not all men will express pleasure by grunting or moaning. He could be the type who internalizes his pleasure. Maybe he communicates his pleasure by going into a meditation state where he is still and non verbal.

"I am not a mind reader! How do you expect me to know what you want if you don't communicate it?" This complaint has spewed out of the mouths of many women. Well, in this particular case, men are deliberately not communicating. Many men don't want to have to tell a woman every single thing they want. These men prefer to be with a woman who gets them. They would like a woman who is observant enough to learn their patterns, take the initiative and make decisions on their own, based on what they have observed. Sure, a man could tell you exactly every detail on what he wants but that would take away the thrill. Some men enjoy being surprised. Maybe you have noticed your boyfriend is into video games. The idea behind this is to perhaps buy a video game magazine and find out what are the upcoming hottest games. Cleverly find out if he may be interested in a particular game or type of game. When he least expects it, surprise him by buying him the game as a gift. What you don't want to do is ask him directly. "What do you want for your birthday?" It just looks like you don't have any clue about what he likes and what his interests are. Also, you remove the element of surprise. Look for clues and then take action. A lot of men like the "Mind Reader"

There are certainly tons of different scenarios where women feel men don't communicate. That is a misconception. Men *do* communicate. The underlying issue is more so that men just don't communicate in the same manner as women would like them to. Men and women often think and approach things differently. The key is to learn to accept that men communicate differently. It may be a more daunting task to get men to communicate the way you would like them to, as opposed to

just becoming more acquainted with the way they

already do.

CHAPTER 10

WHY DO BOYS HAVE A HARD TIME

TRUSTING?

It boils down to one small four letter word: FEAR.

One of the main reasons boys have a hard time

trusting is due to fear. What, exactly, are boys

fearful of? Well, there are a number of reasons but

lets address a few of the more common ones.

A man that has been severely hurt in a previous

relationship can often be traumatized and fearful of

trusting again. Perhaps he was cheated on. He will

now be reluctant to trust another woman for fear

that he will make the same mistake twice and his heart will be broken once again.

Contrary to popular belief, men can be extremely sensitive. While the exterior may be hard, the interior is quite vulnerable. This is one of the major concerns for men. Many fear that if they expose their vulnerabilities, it can be used against them at a later point. They fear that their loved one may expose their intimate feelings to a best friend or family member. They fear that eventually, it may become ammunition used as a low blow in a heated argument. Many men are extremely reluctant to give a woman that level of power and trust.

In the case of successful men, many have a hard

time trusting women because they fear that most women are not truly attracted to them. They believe women are more attracted to their success and the lifestyle that comes with it. This also pertains to men who are public figures.

I remember a friend who happened to be an entertainer. He thought he had a solid, fool-proof plan for finding love as a celebrity. His idea was to go to a remote location in the world where there's no television and find a woman who doesn't know who he is. While on a world tour, he did just that. He came back bragging that he'd found his wife and he was making arrangements for her to come back to the states and live with him. Shortly after her arrival, they got married. Every thing appeared to be fine. Coincidently after she got her green card, which allowed her permanent residence in the states, she filed for a divorce. The divorce was pretty ugly because she also sued him for half of his net worth, which took him a lifetime to achieve. He resented that because she only knew him for 18 months. He was upset about the money and the fact that she may have married him just to gain residence in the U.S. What really turned his stomach happened at the attorney's office during the divorce mediation. She looked him dead in his eyes and said, "I never loved you." After that statement and his divorce, he vowed "I will never trust another woman so long as I live!"

Another reason why boys have a hard time

trusting is due to what I refer to as the Mirror-Reflection Complex. The Mirror-Reflection Complex is when a man accuses or believes that his partner is engaging in, or capable of engaging in, exactly the same inappropriate behaviors and activities as he does. When you're at work, he cheats with the neighbor, so he doesn't trust you at home when he's at work. On the computer, he flirts online, so he doesn't trust you when you're using your computer. He can't trust himself with a female friend, so he doesn't trust you enough to have male friends. So on and so forth. Basically, he doesn't trust you because he believes you are a mirror reflection of his inappropriate behaviors. In actuality, he doesn't trust himself so how can he trust you?

CONCLUSION

This book is certainly not the end-all answer.

However, I have concluded my leg of the relay

race. I encourage all to take the baton and continue

running. Continue asking and exploring. Continue

having those heart-to-heart, open discussions,

anytime and anywhere; in the living room;

coffee shops; lecture halls or on your favorite

blogs. Together, we can collectively have a better

understanding and more insight into the age old

question, "Why do boys...?"

www.ingramcontent.com/pod-product-compliance
Lightning Source LLC
LaVergne TN
LVHW022317080426
835509LV00036B/2123